ETSY FOR BEGINNERS

A Step-by-Step Guide to Setting Up, Optimizing, and Marketing Your Etsy Shop

The Wealth Publisher

CONTENT

1. Introduction to Etsy and the world of online selling
2. Setting up and optimizing your Etsy shop
3. Creating effective product listings
4. Photography and styling tips for Etsy products
5. Building a loyal customer base on Etsy
6. Utilizing SEO and keywords in your Etsy listings
7. Marketing and promoting your Etsy shop
8. Managing Your Etsy Shop and Staying Organized
9. Dealing with Challenges and Overcoming Obstacles
10. Growing Your Etsy Shop and Expanding Your Business
11. Conclusion

INTRODUCTION

Welcome to "Etsy for Beginners: The Ultimate Guide to Setting up, Optimizing, and Marketing Your Etsy Shop for Success". In this book, we will be diving into the world of online selling and giving you all the tips, tricks, and strategies you need to set up and run a successful Etsy shop. Whether you're a complete beginner or you've been dabbling in online sales for a while, this guide is designed to provide you with the knowledge and tools you need to take your Etsy shop to the next level.

In this introduction, we'll be taking a closer look at what Etsy is and how it can benefit you as a seller. We'll also be previewing the topics that we'll be covering throughout the book, including setting up and optimizing your Etsy shop, creating effective product listings, marketing and promoting your shop, and more.

But before we dive into the nitty-gritty details, let me share a bit about my own experience as an Etsy seller. Like many of you, I was once a complete beginner when it came to online sales. But through trial and error, research, and a lot of hard work, I was able to turn my small Etsy shop into a thriving business. And now, I'm excited to share all that I've learned with you in this guide.

So let's get started! Let's explore the world of Etsy and learn how to turn your passion into a successful business.

CHAPTER 1
Introduction to Etsy and the world of online selling

Etsy is an online marketplace that allows individuals and small businesses to sell their handmade, vintage, and unique goods to customers all around the world. It was founded in 2005 and has since grown to become one of the largest online marketplaces for handmade and vintage items.

One of the great things about Etsy is that it is a platform that is accessible to anyone. Whether you're a stay-at-home mom, a retiree, or a student, you can start an Etsy shop and begin selling your goods. It's also an affordable option for those who want to start their own business as there are very little upfront costs involved. All you need is a computer, an internet connection, and a little bit of creativity.

When you open an Etsy shop, you'll be joining a community of over 60 million buyers and sellers from around the world. This means that you'll have access to a huge audience of potential customers, which can be a huge advantage if you're just starting out.

There are a few things that you'll need to know before you start your Etsy shop. First, you'll need to create an account, which is a quick and easy process. Once your account is set up, you can start creating your listings. This is where you'll be able to upload photos of your products, write descriptions, and set prices.

It's important to note that Etsy is a marketplace for handmade, vintage, and unique goods. This means that you can't sell mass-produced items or items that are made using commercial patterns or templates. However, there are some exceptions to this rule, such as vintage items that are at least 20 years old or handmade items that are made using commercial patterns or templates.

When it comes to selling on Etsy, there are a few different options available. You can choose to sell items on a per-item basis, which is the most common option. This means that you'll be charged a listing fee for each item that you sell, as well as a transaction fee when the item sells. Another option is to open a shop subscription, which allows you to list a certain number of items for a monthly fee.

In addition to the listing and transaction fees, there are also a few other costs that you'll need to take into account when you're starting an Etsy shop. These include the cost of materials, the cost of shipping, and the cost of any other expenses that you may incur, such as photography or advertising.

Overall, Etsy is a great platform for anyone looking to start their own business. It's accessible, affordable, and offers a wide audience of potential customers. By following the tips and strategies outlined in this guide, you'll be well on your way to creating a successful Etsy shop that will stand out in this competitive market.

In the next chapter, we will delve into the specifics of setting up and optimizing your Etsy shop. We will cover important topics such as choosing a shop name, creating an attractive shop banner, and crafting a compelling shop story to help you stand out in this competitive market.

CHAPTER 2
Setting up and Optimizing your Etsy Shop

Congratulations on taking the first step to starting your own Etsy shop! In this chapter, we'll be diving into the nitty-gritty details of setting up and optimizing your shop so that it stands out from the crowd. First things first, you'll need to choose a shop name. This is the name that will appear at the top of your shop page and in your shop's URL. Think of something that is catchy and easy to remember. It can be your name, a play on words or something that relates to your products. Just make sure it's not already taken! You can use websites such as Shopify's business name generator, Namelix or NameMesh that generate a variety of shop names based on the category of your product and business. There are also AI-based websites such as BrandBucket, that suggest some really unique business names.

Next, you'll want to create an attractive shop banner. This is the image that will appear at the top of your shop page and it's your chance to make a great first impression. Make sure that the banner is visually appealing and relevant to your shop. You can use a photo of your products or a design that represents your brand. You can also use design tools such as Canva, Adobe Spark or even Etsy's own design tool to create a professional looking banner.

Now that your banner is all set, it's time to craft a compelling shop story. This is your chance to tell customers about your shop, your products and yourself. Make it personal, be funny and interactive. Tell them about your journey, your inspiration and what makes your shop unique. Remember, people buy from people they like, so show them your personality and let them get to know you.

You'll also want to make sure that your shop policies are clearly stated. This includes information about shipping, returns, and payment methods. Be clear and concise, and make sure that your policies are easy to find. You can use pre-made templates for your shop policies which you can easily find online.

Another important aspect of setting up your Etsy shop is to organize your listings into sections. This will make it easier for customers to find what they're looking for and will also make your shop look more professional. You can use Etsy's built-in sections feature or you can even use apps such as Marmalead or TagEZ to help you organize your listings.

Finally, make sure your shop is search engine optimized (SEO) for Etsy. This means that you should use keywords in your titles, tags and descriptions. This will help your shop appear higher in search results when customers are searching for items that are similar to yours. You can use tools such as Marmalead or Google Keyword Planner to help you research keywords.

Now that your shop is all set up and optimized, it's time to start creating product listings. But before you do, let's take a quick break and do some stretches. Trust me, your fingers will thank you later.

Creating effective product listings is the key to success on Etsy, and in the next chapter, we'll be diving deep into the details of how to do just that. From writing compelling descriptions to taking great product photos, we'll cover all the essential elements of creating a listing that will help you make more sales.

CHAPTER 3
Creating Effective Product Listings

Now that your Etsy shop is set up and optimized, it's time to start creating product listings. In this chapter, we'll be diving deep into the details of how to create listings that will help you make more sales.

First and foremost, it's essential to have high-quality product photos. Customers can't hold or touch the items they're buying online, so your photos are their only way of getting a sense of what the product looks like. Make sure that your photos are clear, well-lit, and show the product from different angles. Use a plain background and make sure that the product is the focus of the picture. Additionally, you can also use photo editing tools such as Lightroom, Canva or even Etsy's own photo editing tool to enhance your photos.

Next, you'll want to write compelling product descriptions. Your product descriptions should be clear, concise, and informative. Make sure to include all the important details such as measurements, materials, and care instructions. You can also add a personal touch by telling a story or including the inspiration behind the product. Use active voice and descriptive language to make the product more appealing to potential buyers.

Another important aspect of creating effective product listings is to use keywords. Make sure that you're using relevant keywords in your titles, tags, and descriptions. This will help your listings appear higher in search results when customers are searching for items that are similar to yours. Also, make sure your keyword is used in a natural way, don't stuff it in your title or description. Additionally, using long-tail keywords, which are more specific and targeted, can also help in increasing your visibility in search results.

One of the most underrated yet important aspect of creating effective product listing is pricing your product correctly. Make sure that your prices are competitive and fair. You can also use tools such as Terapeak, to research the prices of similar products on Etsy. Additionally, consider offering bundle deals or discounts for multiple items to entice customers to buy more.

Another important aspect of creating effective product listings is to use multiple images for each listing. Etsy allows you to upload up to 10 images per listing, so make sure to take advantage of this feature. This will give customers a better idea of what the product looks like, and it will also give you the opportunity to show different angles, features, and uses of the product. Additionally, you can also use lifestyle images to showcase how the product can be used in different settings, which can help in increasing the appeal of the product to potential buyers.

It's also important to keep your listings up to date. Make sure that your inventory is accurate and that your listings are current. If a product is out of stock or if you've made changes to a product, make sure to update the listing accordingly. This will help in avoiding any confusion or disappointment for customers.

In conclusion, creating effective product listings is the key to success on Etsy. By following these tips and strategies, you'll be able to create listings that are visually appealing, informative, and optimized for search. With high-quality photos, compelling descriptions, and effective pricing and promotion, you'll be able to increase your visibility, attract more customers, and ultimately make more sales.

CHAPTER 4
Photography & Styling Tips for Etsy Products

As an Etsy seller, having high-quality product photos is essential to make your listings stand out and attract more customers. In this chapter, we'll be discussing different photography and styling tips that will help you take better product photos for your Etsy listings.

First, it's important to have good lighting when taking product photos. Natural light is always the best option, so try to take your photos near a window or outside if possible. If natural light is not available, you can use photography lighting equipment such as softboxes or ring lights to achieve a similar effect.

Next, pay attention to composition and angle when taking your photos. Try to take your photos from different angles to show different features of the product. Additionally, use the rule of thirds when composing your photos for a more visually appealing result.

Styling your product is also an important aspect of taking great product photos. Consider using props or backgrounds that complement your product.

For example, if you're selling jewelry, you can use a velvet background or a model wearing the jewelry to showcase how it will look when worn.

Another tip is to create a consistent look and feel for your photos. This can be achieved by using similar backgrounds, lighting, and styling for all your photos. This will help to establish a cohesive brand image and make your shop appear more professional.

Consider also adding a lifestyle image to your product listing. This is a photo that shows your product in use, like a jewelry on a person's hand or a plant in a pot. This helps customers to visualize the product in their own life, which can help increase the appeal of the product.

Finally, don't be afraid to experiment and try new things. Photography and styling is an art, and there are no hard and fast rules. So, take the time to experiment with different lighting, angles, and styling techniques to find what works best for your products and your brand.

In conclusion, having high-quality product photos is essential for an Etsy shop. By following these photography and styling tips, you'll be able to take better product photos that will help your listings stand out and attract more customers. Additionally, you can also find many photography tutorials and styling ideas on the internet, such as on photography blogs, YouTube channels, and online photography courses, which can help you improve your photography skills and take better product photos for your Etsy shop.

Remember to keep experimenting and trying new things to find what works best for your products and your brand.

CHAPTER 5
Building a Strong Customer Base on Etsy

One of the keys to success on Etsy is building a strong customer base. In this chapter, we'll be discussing different strategies to help you attract, engage, and retain customers on Etsy.

First, it's important to provide excellent customer service. This includes being responsive to customer inquiries, offering a hassle-free return policy and shipping items on time. Positive reviews and word-of-mouth recommendations can help attract new customers to your shop. Go above and beyond for your customers, whether it's adding a personal touch to the packaging, or providing detailed instructions on how to use your products. This will create a memorable experience for your customers, and they'll be more likely to return to your shop.

Next, consider offering a loyalty program or rewards program for customers who make repeat purchases. This can include things like discounts, free shipping or exclusive products. This not only helps retain existing customers, but it can also attract new customers who are looking for rewards or incentives. Create a loyalty program that is easy to join and participate in, and make sure to communicate it effectively to your customers.

Another strategy is to engage with your customers through social media and email marketing. Use platforms like Instagram, Facebook, and email newsletters to keep customers updated on new products, promotions and sales. This helps keep your shop top of mind and attract repeat customers. Create engaging content that showcases your products and your brand, and use it to connect with your customers.

You can also offer a referral program for customers who refer their friends and family to your shop. This can include discounts or free products for both the referrer and the new customer. This can be a powerful way to attract new customers, as people trust recommendations from friends and family more than any other form of advertising.

Finally, consider collaborating with influencers or other Etsy sellers to expand your reach and attract new customers. This can include things like hosting giveaways or creating a limited-time product collection together. Collaboration can help you tap into new audiences, and it can also help you establish new partnerships and relationships that will benefit your shop in the long run.

In conclusion, building a strong customer base on Etsy is essential for long-term success. By providing excellent customer service, offering rewards and incentives, engaging with customers through social media and email marketing, and collaborating with other sellers and influencers, you can attract, engage, and retain customers on Etsy. Remember, a strong customer base is not only important for making sales, but it's also essential for building a loyal community of customers that will support your shop for years to come.

CHAPTER 6

Utilizing SEO and Keywords in Your Etsy Listings

One of the keys to success on Etsy is making sure that your shop and products are easily discoverable by potential customers. In this chapter, we'll be discussing how to utilize SEO and keywords to optimize your Etsy listings and increase visibility in search results.

To begin with, understand the importance of SEO and keywords. Search Engine Optimization (SEO) is the practice of optimizing your website or online content to rank higher in search engine results pages (SERPs). This is important because the higher your products rank in search results, the more likely they are to be seen and purchased by potential customers. Keywords, on the other hand, are the words and phrases that people use to search for products on Etsy. By including the right keywords in your listings, you can increase your chances of appearing in search results for those keywords.

First, research relevant keywords for your products. Use tools such as Google's Keyword Planner or Ahrefs to find the keywords that people are searching for when looking for products like yours. Make sure to include these keywords in your listing title, tags, and description.

Next, optimize your listing title and tags. Your title should be descriptive, concise and contain relevant keywords. Use tags to provide additional information about your product and its characteristics. Avoid using generic tags such as "handmade" or "gift" that don't provide any specific information about your product.

Another strategy is to create unique and compelling product descriptions. Use descriptive language and active voice to make your product stand out. Provide all necessary information about the product, including measurements, materials, and care instructions. Don't forget to include keywords in your description, but make sure to use them in a natural way, don't stuff it in the description.

In addition, use images that are well-lit, clear, and show the product from different angles. Make sure to use high-resolution images and use a plain background to make the product stand out.

Finally, keep your listings up-to-date. Make sure that your inventory is accurate and that your listings are current. If a product is out of stock or if you've made changes to a product, make sure to update the listing accordingly.

By following these strategies, you can optimize your Etsy listings and increase visibility in search results, which will help attract more customers to your shop and increase sales. Additionally, it is important to continually monitor and optimize your listings, as SEO and keyword trends are constantly changing.

CHAPTER 7
Marketing and Promoting Your Etsy Shop

One of the keys to success on Etsy is making sure that your shop and products are seen by potential customers. In this chapter, we'll be discussing different strategies for marketing and promoting your Etsy shop to attract more customers and increase sales.

First, utilize social media to promote your shop and products. Platforms like Instagram, Facebook, and Twitter are great for showcasing your products, engaging with customers, and building your brand. Share high-quality images of your products, create engaging captions, and use relevant hashtags to reach a wider audience.

Next, consider using Etsy Ads to promote your shop and products. Etsy Ads allows you to create targeted campaigns to reach potential customers on and off Etsy. You can target specific keywords, demographics, and even specific items, which can help increase visibility of your shop and products.

You can also use search analytics to monitor the performance of your shop and products on Etsy. Etsy provides analytics tools that allow you to track metrics such as views, favorites, and sales. Use this data to identify which products are performing well and which ones are not, and adjust your marketing strategies accordingly.

Another strategy is to participate in online communities and forums related to your products. This can include things like Etsy teams and online marketplaces. This is a great way to connect with potential customers, share your products and build relationships with other sellers.

You can also use influencer marketing to reach a new audience. Partner with influencers who align with your brand and product offerings and have a large following on social media. They can help promote your products to their audience and attract new customers to your shop.

Finally, consider using custom web addresses offered by Etsy to promote your shop. Etsy allows you to create a custom web address for your shop, which makes it easy for customers to find and remember your shop. This can help increase visibility of your shop and make it more professional.

Another strategy to increase sales is to offer promotions and discounts to attract new customers. This can include things like free shipping, buy one get one deals or discounts on bulk purchases. Make sure to communicate these promotions effectively through social media, email marketing, and in-shop announcements.

In addition, use the above-mentioned tools and strategies to create effective email marketing campaigns. Use email campaigns to promote new products, sales, and upcoming events. Make sure to segment your email list to target specific groups of customers.

Overall, there are many different ways to market and promote your Etsy shop to increase sales. Utilizing social media, Etsy Ads, search analytics, participating in online communities, influencer marketing, custom web addresses, and email marketing can all be effective strategies. It's important to experiment and find the strategies that work best for your shop and products.

CHAPTER 8
Managing Your Etsy Shop and Staying Organized

Managing your Etsy shop and staying organized is crucial to the success of your business. In this chapter, we'll be discussing different strategies for managing your shop and staying organized to increase efficiency and productivity.

First, create a schedule for managing your shop. This can include tasks such as listing new products, responding to customer messages, and processing orders. By creating a schedule, you can make sure that all of your tasks are completed in a timely manner, and you don't miss anything important.

Next, use tools such as spreadsheets, calendars, and to-do lists to stay organized. This will help you keep track of your inventory, sales, and expenses. Additionally, use accounting software to help you manage your finances and stay on top of your expenses.

Another strategy is to use shipping and fulfillment services to save time and increase efficiency. Services like Shipstation and SendOwl can help you automate your shipping process and make it easier to manage your orders.

You can also use customer relationship management (CRM) software to manage your customer interactions and sales. CRM software allows you to keep track of customer interactions, sales and feedback, which can help you improve your customer service and increase sales.

Finally, make sure to take breaks and manage your time effectively. Running an Etsy shop can be demanding, and it's important to take breaks and manage your time effectively to avoid burnout.

In conclusion, managing your Etsy shop and staying organized is crucial to the success of your business. By creating a schedule, using tools such as spreadsheets, calendars and to-do lists, using shipping and fulfillment services, utilizing CRM software, and effectively managing your time, you can increase efficiency and productivity in your shop, which will help you increase sales and grow your business.

CHAPTER 9

Dealing with Challenges & Overcoming Obstacles

Starting and running an Etsy shop can be challenging, and it's important to be prepared to deal with obstacles and challenges that may arise. In this chapter, we'll be discussing different strategies for dealing with challenges and overcoming obstacles in your Etsy shop.

First, it's important to be prepared for seasonal fluctuations in sales. Many Etsy shops experience a slowdown in sales during certain times of the year, such as summer or the holiday season. To prepare for these fluctuations, create a plan to increase sales during slow periods, such as offering promotions or creating a sale section in your shop.

Another common challenge for Etsy shop owners is dealing with competition. To stand out from the competition, make sure to have high-quality images and descriptions for your products, provide excellent customer service, and use effective marketing strategies.

Another obstacle that you may face is dealing with negative reviews or customer complaints. It's important to respond to negative reviews in a timely and professional manner, and to use the feedback to improve your shop and customer service.

You may also face challenges related to taxes and regulations. It's important to stay informed about the regulations and tax laws that apply to your Etsy shop, and to be prepared to file taxes and keep records accordingly.

Finally, it's important to have a plan in place for dealing with unexpected events such as the COVID-19 pandemic. This might include things like updating your business plan, diversifying your product offerings, and finding new ways to reach customers.

In conclusion, running an Etsy shop can be challenging, and it's important to be prepared to deal with obstacles and challenges that may arise. By preparing for seasonal fluctuations in sales, standing out from the competition, dealing with negative reviews and customer complaints, staying informed about taxes and regulations, and having a plan in place for unexpected events, you can be better prepared to deal with any challenges that may arise in your Etsy shop.

CHAPTER 10

Growing Your Etsy Shop and Expanding Your Business

Congratulations on establishing a successful Etsy shop! Now it's time to take it to the next level and start thinking about ways to grow and expand your business. In this chapter, we'll be discussing different strategies for growing your Etsy shop and taking it to new heights. But before we get into the nitty-gritty, let's take a moment to appreciate how far you've come. You're a boss now, running your own Etsy shop like a pro! High-five!

Okay, now let's get down to business. First, consider diversifying your product offerings. This can include adding new products, expanding into new product categories, or even offering custom-made products. By diversifying your product offerings, you can attract new customers and increase sales. And let's be real, who doesn't love a little variety in their life?

Next, consider opening a second Etsy shop or starting a website to expand your reach and increase visibility. Having multiple channels for customers to find and purchase your products can help you attract new customers and increase sales. Plus, having a website gives you more freedom to showcase your products and create a unique brand identity.

Another strategy is to collaborate with other Etsy shop owners, influencers, and brands. Collaborating with others can help you tap into new audiences, and it can also help you establish new partnerships and relationships that will benefit your shop in the long run. Plus, it's always fun to work with other boss ladies and gents!

You can also use email marketing and social media to increase visibility and attract new customers. Use email campaigns to promote new products, sales, and upcoming events. Make sure to segment your email list to target specific groups of customers. And don't forget to post on Instagram, Facebook and Twitter to keep your customers updated on new products, promotions and sales.

Finally, consider offering wholesale options to increase your sales. Wholesale options allow other businesses and retailers to purchase your products at a discounted rate, which can help increase your sales and expand your reach.

In conclusion, growing your Etsy shop and expanding your business is an exciting and rewarding journey. By diversifying your product offerings, expanding your reach, collaborating with others, using email marketing and social media, and offering wholesale options, you can take your Etsy shop to new heights and achieve your business goals. Remember to always have fun and enjoy the journey!

CHAPTER 11
Conclusion

Congratulations on making it to the final chapter of this guide! By now, you should have a good understanding of how to start and run a successful Etsy shop. In this chapter, we'll be summarizing the key points discussed in the previous chapters and providing some final thoughts and recommendations for those looking to start their own Etsy shop. But before we dive in, let's take a moment to give ourselves a pat on the back for making it this far. You're one step closer to running your own successful Etsy shop, and that's something to celebrate!

In summary, starting and running an Etsy shop requires a lot of hard work and dedication, but with the right strategies and tools, it can be a highly rewarding experience. We've discussed the importance of finding the right niche, creating a strong brand, providing excellent customer service, and utilizing marketing and promotion strategies to increase visibility and sales. We've also discussed some of the common challenges and obstacles that Etsy shop owners may face, and provided strategies for dealing with them.

As you move forward with your Etsy shop, keep in mind the importance of consistency and persistence. Building a successful Etsy shop takes time, and it's important to stay dedicated and committed to your business. Keep experimenting with new strategies, and be open to trying new things. Remember, the best way to predict the future of your Etsy shop is to create it.

Another important point to remember is that the journey of an entrepreneur is not always an easy one, and it's important to have a support system. Surround yourself with people who will encourage and support you. It's also important to take care of yourself, both physically and mentally. Running a business can be demanding, and it's essential to take breaks and make time for yourself.

In conclusion, this guide is a great starting point for anyone who wants to start and run a successful Etsy shop. Remember to be persistent, be creative, and enjoy the journey of building your business. With the right strategies, tools, and a positive attitude, you can achieve your business goals and create a successful Etsy shop.

www.ingramcontent.com/pod-product-compliance
Lightning Source LLC
Chambersburg PA
CBHW050318220526
45465CB00005B/2039